DOMINOES

Fraser Valley Regional Library

Sherlock Holmes:
The Dying Detective
Sir Arthur Conan Doyle

D0792890

Founder Editors: Bill Bowler and Sue Parminter

Text adaptation by Lesley Thompson

Illustrated by Giorgio Bacchin

Sir Arthur Conan Doyle (1859–1930), born in Edinburgh, Scotland, is best known as the creator of Sherlock Holmes. He started writing after working as a doctor, and soon became one of the world's best-known authors. The Sherlock Holmes stories *The Blue Diamond*, *The Emerald Crown*, *The Norwood Mystery*, *The Sign of Four*, *The Top-Secret Plans*, and *The Speckled Band* are also available as Dominoes.

OXFORD
UNIVERSITY PRESS

OXFORD
UNIVERSITY PRESS

Great Clarendon Street, Oxford, OX2 6DP, United Kingdom

Oxford University Press is a department of the University of Oxford.
It furthers the University's objective of excellence in research, scholarship,
and education by publishing worldwide. Oxford is a registered trade
mark of Oxford University Press in the UK and in certain other countries

ISBN: 978 0 19 424972 0   Book
ISBN: 978 0 19 462236 3   Book and Audio pack
Audio not available separately

Printed in China

This book is printed on paper from certified and well-managed sources

ACKNOWLEDGEMENTS

Illustrations by: Giorgio Bacchin/Beehive Illustration.

The publisher would like to thank the following for permission to reproduce photographs:
Alamy Stock Photo p.15 (hansom cab/Amoret Tanner); Getty Images p.11 (Map Of The
Centre Of London, Great Britain, 1899/Universal History Archive/UIG); Kobal Collection
pp.25 (*Sherlock Holmes* 2009/Silver Pictures), 25 (*Adventures of Sherlock Holmes* 1939/Twentieth
Century Fox), 25 (*Mr Holmes* 2015/AI-Film/See-Saw Films/Archer Gray/BBC Films);
Rex Shutterstock pp.24 (Benedict Cumberbatch/Rex), 25 (Jeremy Brett/ITV).

Contents

Story Characters

Sherlock Holmes

Doctor Watson

Story Characters

Mrs Hudson

Inspector Morton

Mr Culverton Smith

Victor Savage

BEFORE READING

1 Match the words in the box with the characters. Use a dictionary to help you.

a farmer in the Far East   a young man   an important police officer
Holmes's best friend   Holmes's servant   Watson's best friend

a Victor Savage is ....

b Sherlock Holmes is ....

c Mrs Hudson is ....

d Inspector Morton is ....

e Mr Culverton Smith is ....

f Doctor Watson is ....

2 What do you think happens in the story? Write the names from Activity 1.

a .... asks Watson to help Holmes.

b .... is killed.

c .... wants to kill Holmes.

d .... is very ill.

e .... asks Culverton Smith to help.

f .... arrests someone for murder.

1. Holmes is ill

It is 1890 in London. At 221b Baker Street, Mrs Hudson, Sherlock Holmes's **servant**, is **sad**. Things are very bad. Holmes is dying!

'Three days now, and he is worse!' she thinks.

Mrs Hudson likes Holmes very much but she is also a little afraid of him. He is different. He has **strange** visitors and they come at all hours of the day and night. His rooms have many strange things in them. But he is very nice to Mrs Hudson. She **respects** him and she does not want to lose him.

'I must visit **Dr** Watson,' she thinks. 'He can help.'

At this time, Dr Watson is living in a different street in London. Mrs Hudson goes quickly to his rooms.

'Dr Watson!' she cries when the doctor opens the door to her. 'Please come with me. It's Mr Holmes. He's dying!'

servant a person who works for someone rich

sad not happy

strange not usual

respect to think that someone is good

Dr, doctor this person helps people when they are ill

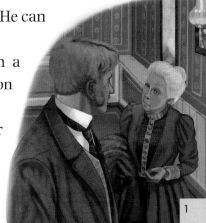

ill, illness being not well

cab a car pulled by a horse

river a long line of water

'What?' Watson cries. 'I know nothing about this!'

'He doesn't want a doctor but you must come, sir. After three days, he's very, very **ill**. He's saying strange things. I'm afraid for him. You must be quick!'

Watson gets his coat and bag and they leave the house. In the **cab**, he asks Mrs Hudson some more questions.

'I can't tell you much, sir. Lately, Mr Holmes is working in Rotherhithe, near the **river**. He comes home and he brings this **illness** with him. He's much worse now. Can he live through this?'

READING CHECK

Choose the correct word to complete these sentences.

a Sherlock Holmes lives with his *cat / servant*.

b Holmes is ill and Mrs Hudson is *happy / sad*.

c Holmes has some strange *visitors / animals*.

d Mrs Hudson *respects / doesn't like* Holmes.

e Watson lives in a different *town / house* to Holmes.

f Lately, Holmes's work is near the *river / garden*.

g Mrs Hudson and Watson go by *cab / train* to visit Holmes.

h Perhaps Holmes is *driving / dying*.

GUESS WHAT

What do you think happens in the next chapter? Tick the boxes.

a Watson talks to Holmes.

b Mrs Hudson sees Holmes in the street.

c Holmes gets out of bed.

d Watson hits Holmes in the face.

2. Watson cannot help

detective a man or woman who finds criminals

fever a person with this is very hot and ill

voice you talk or sing with this

weak not strong

poor something you say when you feel sorry for someone

towards nearer

When they arrive at Baker Street on that dark, November day, Holmes is alive. But Watson is afraid for his friend. The **detective**'s face is yellow, and his eyes are red with **fever**. His hands move without stopping. When he speaks, his **voice** is **weak**.

'Well, Watson, bad days are here, I think.' He smiles weakly.

'My **poor** man!' cries Watson and he moves **towards** the bed.

'Don't come near me!'

'But why? I only want to help.'

'I know, but you can't help me. My illness is from the Far East and it's very **contagious**.'

'I'm a doctor,' says Watson quietly. 'These things don't matter to me.'

'Don't move, and I can talk to you. If not, you must leave the room now.'

contagious an illness which is easy to get

Holmes looks at Watson with fever in his eyes.

'I can't **trust** you with this, Watson. You know nothing of these strange illnesses. Do you know about Tapanuli fever, for example? Or the black Formosa fever? No, you don't. You aren't a **specialist**. I'm sorry to say this, but I must see a specialist.'

Watson is not happy at these words, but he also respects the detective.

'Very well, Holmes. Dr Ainstree, the best specialist in these illnesses, is now in London. I'm going to him now.'

Watson walks towards the door. Suddenly, Holmes is out of bed. He goes quickly to the door and **locks** it. Then he goes very slowly back to bed. Watson looks at his friend in **shock**. What is the matter with Holmes?

READING CHECK

Write *Holmes* or *Watson* to complete the sentences.

a ....Holmes...... is very ill when his friend arrives.

b .... wants to go nearer the bed.

c .... says, 'This illness is contagious.'

d .... is not a specialist in strange illnesses.

e .... wants to bring a specialist to the house.

f .... locks the door of his room.

GUESS WHAT

What happens in the next chapter? Tick a box to finish each sentence.

a Holmes...

1 ☐ gives Watson the name of a specialist.　**2** ☐ eats and drinks a lot.　**3** ☐ plays the violin.

b Watson...

1 ☐ goes out through the window.　**2** ☐ finds something interesting on the table.　**3** ☐ suddenly feels very ill.

3. Holmes is worse

Holmes cries excitedly, 'Stay here, Watson! I've got the **key**! What time is it? Four o'clock? At six o'clock you can go, but not before!'

Watson looks at his friend sadly.

'Holmes, this illness is doing strange things to your head. But I can wait until six.'

'Good! One more thing, Watson. Don't bring that man, Ainstree. Now, perhaps I can sleep a little.'

Watson waits, looking at the pictures and books in the room. On a table, he sees a little black and white **box**. 'That's interesting,' he thinks. He moves his hand towards it. Suddenly, a **terrible** cry comes from the bed.

'Stop, Watson! Don't move my things. I don't like it. Sit down, man! I need to sleep!'

key you use this to lock a door

box a square thing which you put things in

terrible very bad

At six o'clock, Holmes says, 'Let's have some **light**, Watson. But only a little! Put the box near me. Not with your hands! Use your **handkerchief**! That's right. Now, you can go to Mr Culverton Smith of 13 Lower **Burke** Street.'

'But who is this man, Holmes? I don't know the name.'

'He isn't a doctor. He has a **plantation** in **Sumatra** but he's visiting London. He knows this illness well because his workers often have it.

Things are not good between us. Smith's **nephew**, Victor Savage, is dead. There is something wrong about his terrible death. I don't trust Smith and he knows it. But only he can help me. There is one more thing. Don't come back with him. You must be here before him. This is very important, Watson.'

light this stops a place being dark

handkerchief a small square white cloth

Burke /bɜrk/

plantation a big farm in a hot country

Sumatra /sʊˈmɑtrə/

nephew your brother or sister's son

Watson takes the key and he goes into the street. He sees **Inspector** Morton of **Scotland Yard**.

'How is Mr Holmes, sir?' Morton asks.

'He's very ill,' Watson answers.

Morton smiles strangely. 'I know something about it,' he says.

Watson doesn't understand, but he cannot wait. He gets into a cab and leaves.

READING CHECK

Put these sentences in order. Number them 1–6.

a ☐ Watson meets Inspector Morton in the street.

b ☐ Holmes is angry because Watson is moving his things.

c ☐ Watson sees an interesting box on the table.

d ☐ Holmes asks about the time.

e ☐ Watson leaves the house.

f ☐ Inspector Morton asks about Holmes.

GUESS WHAT

What happens in the next chapter? Circle the words to complete the sentences.

a Watson goes *by cab / on foot* to Culverton Smith's house.

b At first, Culverton Smith *wants / doesn't want* to see Watson.

c Watson tells Culverton Smith about Holmes's *illness / servant*.

d Culverton Smith is *interested / not interested* in Holmes.

e Culverton Smith goes to Holmes's house *without / with* Watson.

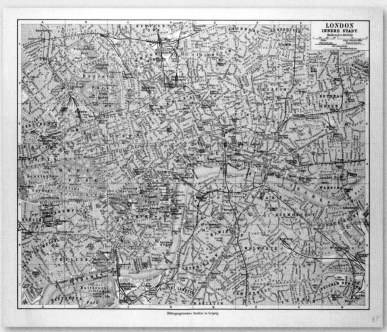

4. The specialist

At 13 Lower Burke Street, a servant answers the door. Watson goes into the house. He can hear Culverton Smith's voice.

'Who is Watson? What does he want? I need to work. I cannot see him.'

Watson thinks of Holmes. Quickly he goes into the room. The man in the room stands up from his chair. Watson sees his dark, angry eyes.

'What's this?' the man cries.

'I'm sorry,' says Watson, 'but I can't wait. It's about Mr Sherlock Holmes.'

Culverton Smith's face changes. He watches Watson carefully.

'What about Holmes? How is he?'

'He's very ill.'

Watson sits down. Is that a smile on Smith's face?

'I'm sorry to hear this,' Smith says. 'I don't know Holmes well, but I respect him. We're not very different. He studies **criminals** and I study **microbes**.' He looks at the bottles on the table next to him and laughs.

criminal a bad person who the police are looking for

microbe a very little thing which can make you ill

'Holmes needs you,' Watson says.

'Why? Is his illness from the Far East?'

'Perhaps. His work lately is with people from there.'

'Oh, I see,' Smith smiles. 'How many days is it now?'

'About three.'

'Is he thinking well?'

'Not always.'

'That is bad. I must go and help him.'

Watson remembers Holmes's words. He says, 'I can't go with you. I need to make a visit.'

'Very well,' Smith says. 'I can be there in half an hour.'

READING CHECK

Are these sentences true or false? Tick the boxes.

		True	False
a	Culverton Smith opens the door of his house.	☐	☑
b	Culverton Smith is angry because he is working.	☐	☐
c	When Watson says Holmes's name, everything changes.	☐	☐
d	Culverton Smith asks questions about Holmes's illness.	☐	☐
e	Watson goes to Baker Street with Culverton Smith.	☐	☐
f	Watson must visit Mrs Hudson.	☐	☐

GUESS WHAT

What happens in the next chapter? Tick two boxes.

a ☐ Watson goes behind Holmes's bed.

b ☐ Holmes asks Culverton Smith for money.

c ☐ Culverton Smith talks about Victor Savage.

d ☐ Mrs Hudson calls the police.

5. A killer at Baker Street

Watson runs into Holmes's room.

'Is he coming?' Holmes asks.

'Yes, he is.'

'Very good, Watson! Now you must **hide** behind the bed. Don't speak or move. Just listen very carefully.'

Watson hides behind the bed and waits. Soon, he hears Culverton Smith's voice.

'Can you hear me, Holmes?'

'Is that you, Mr Smith?' Holmes says weakly. 'Thank you for coming.'

Smith laughs. 'What's the matter with you, Holmes?'

'It's Victor's illness, I think,'

'Yes! My nephew! Four days ill and he's dead!' Smith laughs again.

'And you are the criminal, Smith.'

'Ah, but you can't **prove** it! And now you need me!'

'Give me water!' Holmes says weakly.

'All right, but only because I want to say something to you. Your illness is from men working near the river, your friend says. But that's wrong. You aren't very quick, are you Holmes?'

'I can't think. You must help me!'

'Think carefully. Think about a box arriving here last Wednesday.'

'A box... yes, I remember now. The **spring** in the box on my hand... the **blood**!'

hide to go where people can't see you

prove to show that something is true

spring a thin metal thing in a watch or clock

blood this is red; you can see it when you cut your hand

16

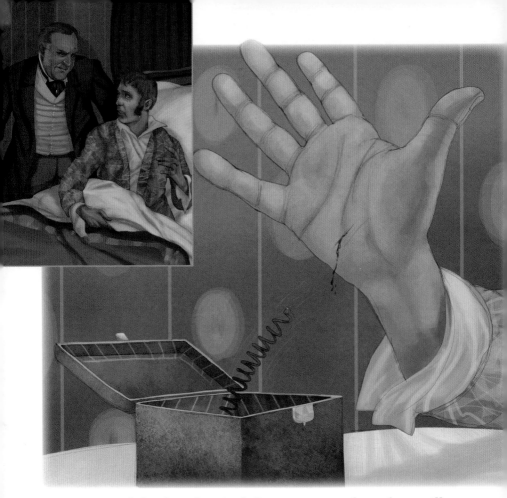

'That's right. And there are microbes of your illness on that spring. This box is the only **proof**, and I'm taking it with me! Now you know the **truth**. Now you can die!'

'More light,' says Holmes weakly. Smith moves and suddenly there is more light in the room. 'What more can I do for you?' Smith asks.

proof a thing which shows that something is true

truth what is true

normally in a usual way

'And more water, please,' Holmes says. But what is happening? Holmes is speaking **normally**. His voice is not weak. Watson hears this and he nearly cries out. He can feel Culverton Smith's shock.

READING CHECK

Correct the mistakes in these sentences.

a Holmes thanks Watson for his visit. .....Culverton Smith......

b Watson is on Holmes's bed. ....

c Culverton Smith is sad about Holmes's illness. ....

d Victor Savage is Culverton Smith's father. ....

e Holmes asks for some milk. ....

f Culverton Smith talks about the little book. ....

g Holmes wants less light. ....

h Suddenly, Watson speaks in a different voice. ....

GUESS WHAT

What happens in the next chapter? Write Holmes, Watson, Culverton Smith, or Inspector Morton.

a ....comes out from behind the bed.
b ....walks into the room.
c .... and ....go to the police station.
d ....tells Watson all about his illness.

6. The truth

'What is this? Aren't you ill?' Culverton Smith asks angrily.

'After three days without food or drink I'm not very well. But I'm much better than you think,' Holmes says in his normal voice. 'Ah, a friend is coming, I think. The light is telling him to come.'

The door opens and Inspector Morton comes in.

'This is your man, Inspector,' Holmes says.

'I **arrest** you for the **murder** of Victor Savage,' Morton says to Smith.

arrest to take (a criminal) to the police station

murder the killing of someone

'He wants my murder, too.' Holmes laughs. 'The proof is in the box in his coat. But don't put your hand on it, Inspector'.

Smith cries, 'You can't prove anything, Holmes!'

'Don't forget my friend, Dr Watson,' Holmes says. 'He can tell an interesting story. Come out, Watson!'

Morton leaves with Culverton Smith. Holmes dresses and then he talks to Watson.

'I'm a good **actor**, Watson. And no food or drink for three days is easy for me. This yellow face is only **make-up**. You can't come near me and not see the truth – so my 'illness' is contagious. Bad light in the room helps with my **act**.

Victor Savage's murder is all about money. Money is more important than family to Culverton Smith. I get some strange things at this house. Happily, I always open them very carefully!

Now we must go to Scotland Yard. After that, I want to sit down with you and eat until midnight!'

READING CHECK

Match the first and second parts of the sentences.

a Culverton Smith is angry   **1** very good actor.

b Holmes drinks   **2** a murderer.

c Inspector Morton knows   **3** with Holmes.

d Morton arrests   **4** very hungry.

e Morton doesn't put his hand   **5** about Culverton Smith.

f Dr Watson comes out   **6** to Scotland Yard.

g Holmes is a   **7** Culverton Smith.

h Culverton Smith is   **8** some water.

i After three days, Holmes feels   **9** from behind the bed.

j Holmes and Watson are going   **10** on the box.

GUESS WHAT

What happens after the story ends? Choose from these ideas, and write your own ideas, too.

a ☐ Culverton Smith goes back to Sumatra.

b ☐ Watson is angry with Holmes and doesn't speak to him.

c ☐ Mrs Hudson goes to work for Watson.

d ☐ Holmes works with Inspector Morton at Scotland Yard.

e ....

f ....

Project A *Sherlock actors*

Sherlock Holmes is in many films on TV and in the cinema. Read about two different Sherlock actors. Use a dictionary to help you.

1 Read about Benedict Cumberbatch. Complete the table.

Benedict Cumberbatch

Benedict Cumberbatch, born in 1976, is an English actor. He plays Sherlock Holmes on BBC television. His Sherlock is very famous all over the world.

Cumberbatch plays Sherlock in the twenty-first century. Sherlock uses modern technology, for example mobile phones, texting, and computers.

Like Sherlock, Cumberbatch is tall and likes music. He also has a beautiful voice. Cumberbatch cannot play the violin, but on television his Sherlock plays it – badly! Cumberbatch is different to Sherlock because he is married and he has lots of friends. He also likes laughing.

Cumberbatch says, 'Sherlock is not always good to his friend Watson. Watson needs people more than the detective.'

A lot of these Sherlock stories are made in Cardiff, in Wales. It is much cheaper than London!

Name of actor	Benedict Cumberbatch
From	
Born	
Similarities to Holmes	
Differences to Holmes	
Cumberbatch says	Sherlock is not always good to Watson.
Interesting information	

2 **Read the notes in the table and complete the text about Robert Downey Junior.**

Name of actor	Robert Downey Junior
From	New York, USA
Born	1965
Similarities to Holmes	He is a little strange. Likes doing different things. Good at fighting.
Differences to Holmes	American, not English.
Downey Junior says	Watson is an ex-soldier. He likes women. Very different to Holmes.
Interesting information	The films are full of action. Holmes talks less and fights more!

Robert Downey Junior, born in .... is an .... actor. He plays Sherlock Holmes in two films from 2009 and 2011.
Like Sherlock, Downey Junior .... He likes ....
He also likes ....
Downey Junior is not ....
His Doctor Watson is Jude Law, an English actor. Downey Junior says, 'Watson is .... because he ....
In these films, Holmes .... The films are ....

3 **Find out about more famous Sherlock actors on the Internet. How many can you find?**

Project B *A diary entry*

1 **Mrs Hudson writes about Sherlock Holmes's illness in her diary. Read it and correct the mistakes. There are nine more.**

Tuesday

Today Mr Holmes is ~~walking~~ *working* near the river. He comes back at seven o'clock and he is not very well.

What is the matter with him? This evening, he eats and drinks nothing.

Wednesday

Mr Holmes is better today. He isn't eating or drinking anything. He is very ill and I am very happy. What can I do? He is in bed. His eyes are open and he isn't sleeping. He is very hot all the time. He has a terrible fever. I want to call a gardener but Mr Holmes says no. I respect him but he is right this time. He needs to see someone.

Thursday

This is the fourth day and Mr Holmes is not better. His face is all yellow and his eyes are red. What strange illness is this? I am going to see Dr Watson. He can help me and perhaps he can help Mr Holmes, too.

Three days without food or drink. The poor man is driving! Perhaps he is right and this terrible illness comes from the Far West.

Sadly, Dr Watson knows everything about this new illness. He is a bad doctor but he isn't a specialist. We must think carefully.

2 Read this entry from Dr Watson's diary and fill in the gaps with suitable words.

THURSDAY

Mrs Hudson comes to see me today. The poor woman is very sad because Holmes is in **a)** ......bed........., *she says. I go with her by* **b)** .... *to Baker Street.*

I go into Holmes's room and there he is! My poor friend is very ill. His **c)** .... *is very weak and I cannot hear him. His face and hands are a terrible* **d)** .... *colour. He says some very strange things. He isn't thinking well and he has a* **e)** .... *. I'm a doctor so of course I want to help. But Holmes wants to see a* **f)** .... *. He doesn't trust me, his good friend. This is all terrible to me. There are specialists in London, but Holmes doesn't* **g)** .... *to see them. He talks of Mr Culverton Smith. The* **h)** .... *is new to me. He is not a doctor, but a farmer in the Far East. What can he know about Holmes's illness?*

I wait until six o'clock and then I leave for Culverton Smith's **i)** .... *. Perhaps he can help Holmes, after all. He must help him because my poor friend is not just ill. He is* **j)** .... *!*

3 Write a diary entry for another character in the story. Use the diary entries above to help you.

WORD WORK 1

1 Match the words from Chapters 5 and 6 with the pictures.

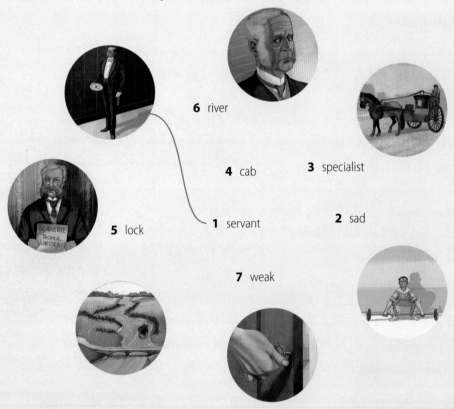

6 river

4 cab   **3** specialist

5 lock   **1** servant   **2** sad

7 weak

2 Unscramble the letters to complete the sentences.

a You're very hot. Have you got a f e v e r? **EVREF**

b With this _ _ _ _ _ _ _ _ you feel cold all the time. **SNESLIL**

c She's a good teacher and the children _ _ _ _ _ _ _ _ her. **TREPECS**

d Is that man dead? Oh, no! What a _ _ _ _ _! **CHOSK**

e He never looks me in the eye. I don't _ _ _ _ _ him. **STURT**

f That child isn't well. He needs a _ _ _ _ _ _ _. **COTROD**

g Don't go near him. Yellow fever is very _ _ _ _ _ _ _ _ _ _ _. **GATONOICSU**

h He's a _ _ _ _ _ _ _ _ man. Nobody understands him. **GARSTEN**

i My _ _ _ _ girl! What is the matter? **ROPO**

WORD WORK 2

1 Complete each sentence with the best word in the box.

inspector	light	microbe	~~nephew~~	terrible

a My young ...*nephew*...... is nine on Saturday.

b John works very hard. He wants to be an ....

c I can't see the words in my book very well. I need more..................... .

d What a.....................noise!

e It is not easy to see a ....because it is very little.

2 These words don't match the pictures. Correct them.

a box

.............*key*.........

b plantation

....

c voice

....

d handkerchief

....

e key

....

f criminal

....

WORD WORK 3

1 Find words from Chapters 5 and 6 in the boxes to match the pictures.

a IHED ...hide... **b** DOBLO .... **c** GRISNP ....

d OCRAT .... **e** EKAM-PU ....

2 Complete the puzzle with different new words from Chapters 5 and 6.

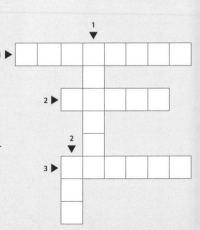

ACROSS

1 I don't n _ _ _ _ _ _ _ eat bread but today is different.

2 You can't say, 'He's the killer'. You need p _ _ _ _.

3 You can a _ _ _ _ _ him, Inspector. He's the killer.

DOWN

1 The m _ _ _ _ _ of someone is a very bad thing.

2 She isn't rich. It's all an a _ _.

GRAMMAR CHECK

Information questions and question words.

We use question words in information questions. We answer these questions by giving some information.

Where is Baker Street?	*In London.*
Why is Mrs Hudson sad?	*Because Holmes is ill.*
How much does Holmes know about Victor's murder?	*A lot.*

1 Complete the information questions with the words in the box.

> ~~How many~~ How much What When
> Where Which Who Why

a Q: ...How many... days are you ill, Holmes?

 A: Three.

b Q: .... is your illness?

 A: Perhaps it is Tapanuli fever.

c Q: .... is your illness from?

 A: The Far East, I think.

d Q: .... do you know about the illness?

 A: Very little.

e Q: .... doctor do you want to see?

 A: I want to see you.

f Q: .... is the best specialist in London?

 A: You are the best.

g Q: .... is the third day of your illness?

 A: Today.

h Q: .... do you want to see me?

 A: Because I am dying.

GRAMMAR CHECK

Present Simple: *Yes* / *No* questions and short answers.

We use auxiliary verbs and *be* (main verb) in *Yes* / *No* questions.

In the short answer, we re-use the auxiliary verb and *be* (main verb).

Do you trust him?   *No, I don't (do not).*

Are Holmes and Watson English?   *Yes, they are.*

2 **Write answers for the questions about the people in the story. Use the short answers in the box.**

No, he doesn't.   No, she can't.   No, she doesn't.   No, they don't.   Yes, it is.
Yes, he can.   Yes, he does.   ~~Yes, she does.~~   Yes, they are.   Yes, they do.

a Does Mrs Hudson work in London? ..Yes,..she..does...........

b Can she help Holmes? ....

c Does she know about Culverton Smith? ....

d Does Watson know a lot about Holmes's illness? ....

e Does Culverton Smith kill his nephew? ....

f Are Holmes and Watson good friends? ....

g Can Inspector Morton arrest Culverton Smith? ....

h Is Holmes's illness an act? ....

i Do Watson and Mrs Hudson respect Holmes? ....

j Do Mrs Hudson and Holmes go to Lower Burke Street? ....

3 **Write short answers for these questions.**

a Is Holmes ill? ...No,..he..isn't...........

b Is Culverton Smith a murderer? ....

c Does Inspector Morton help Holmes? ....

d Can Victor Savage help Holmes? ....

e Are Watson and Culverton Smith friends? ....

f Does Mrs Hudson go to Watson's house? ....

GRAMMAR CHECK

Linkers: *and, but, so,* and *because*

and links two parts of a sentence with the same idea.

Holmes can act and he can play the violin, too.

but links two parts of a sentence with different ideas.

Watson is a doctor but he doesn't know about strange illnesses.

so links two parts of a sentence about the result of something.

Watson doesn't understand Holmes's illness so <u>he visits Culverton Smith.</u>

(result of first part of sentence)

because links two parts of a sentence about the reason for something.

Watson hides behind the bed because <u>he wants to listen to Culverton Smith.</u>

(reason for first part of sentence)

4 Complete the sentences with *and, but, so* or *because.*

a Every afternoon, Holmes reads his books ......*and*...... in the evening he plays the violin.

b Holmes is a good detective .... he isn't always very nice.

c Mrs Hudson goes to see Watson .... Holmes is ill.

d Watson is sad about Holmes .... he goes to see Culverton Smith.

e Watson wants to help Holmes .... he doesn't understand his friend's illness.

f Watson wants to see Culverton Smith now .... he doesn't wait.

g Watson hides behind the bed .... Holmes talks to Culverton Smith.

h The box is proof of murder .... Culverton Smith takes it.

i Holmes can't help Victor Savage .... he can arrest Culverton Smith.

j Watson is very happy .... Holmes is well.

33

DOMINOES Your Choice

Read *Dominoes* for pleasure, or to develop language skills. It's your choice.

Each *Domino* reader includes:
- a good story to enjoy
- integrated activities to develop reading skills and increase vocabulary
- task-based projects – perfect for CEFR portfolios
- contextualized grammar activities

Each *Domino* pack contains a reader, and an excitingly dramatized audio recording of the story

If you liked this *Domino*, read these:

Merlin
Janet Hardy-Gould

'Be careful with Morfran,' Princess Adhan tells her young son, Merlin.

Morfran, the son of the Enchantress Ceridwen, is a bully. Then one day, Merlin drinks one of Ceridwen's magic potions. After this, he can become different animals, see through walls, change the weather, and look into the future. But Morfran is angry with Merlin when Ceridwen dies. Years later, Morfran – now King Vortigern's magician – plans to kill Merlin, the boy with no father. How can Merlin's magic powers help him to fight his old enemy?

Zombie Attack
Lesley Thompson

'Professor Clark's work usually helps people. But this is something new.'

Clark's helper – Tasha Kiara – is telling Chaz – a local TV reporter about the Professor's new serum.

Then an earthquake hits Clark's California lab, and his serum brings dead bodies in the cemetery alive. Soon the zombies attack! What happens to Professor Clark? How can Tasha and Chaz stop the zombies? Who lives and who dies? Read this story and see.

	CEFR	Cambridge Exams	IELTS	TOEFL iBT	TOEIC
Level 3	B1	PET	4.0	57-86	550
Level 2	A2–B1	KET-PET	3.0-4.0	–	390
Level 1	A1–A2	YLE Flyers/KET	3.0	–	225
Starter & Quick Starter	A1	YLE Movers	1.0–2.0	–	–

You can find details and a full list of books and teachers' resources on our website:
www.oup.com/elt/gradedreaders